LOOKING BACK
LIFE WAS BEAUTIFUL

LOOKING BACK
LIFE WAS BEAUTIFUL

A Celebration of Love from the Creators of
Drawings for My Grandchildren

Illustrations by Grandpa Chan
Words by Grandma Marina
Translated by Sophie Bowman

A TarcherPerigee Book

tarcherperigee

an imprint of Penguin Random House LLC
penguinrandomhouse.com

Library of Congress Cataloging-in-Publication Data

Names: Ahn, Kyong Ja, 1942– author. | Lee, Chan Jae, 1942– illustrator.
Title: Looking back life was beautiful: a celebration of love from the
creators of drawings for my grandchildren / illustrations by Grandpa Chan;
words by Grandma Marina; translated by Sophie Bowman.
Description: New York: TarcherPerigee, [2020]
Identifiers: LCCN 2020015707 (print) | LCCN 2020015708 (ebook) |
ISBN 9780593188675 (board) | ISBN 9780593188682 (ebook)
Subjects: LCSH: Lee, Chan Jae, 1942— | Ahn, Kyong Ja, 1942— |
Grandparent and child. | Grandparent and child—Pictorial works. |
Families. | Families—Pictorial works.
Classification: LCC HQ759.9.A423 2020 (print) | LCC HQ759.9 (ebook) |
DDC 306.85—dc23
LC record available at https://lccn.loc.gov/2020015707
LC ebook record available at https://lccn.loc.gov/2020015708

Printed in Germany
1   3   5   7   9   10   8   6   4   2

Book design by Laura K. Corless

Everything is right there in your heart.
It will guide you.

CONTENTS

FOREWORD

Today, as we do every day, we're thinking of what to draw next. We are always searching for inspiration and talking over our ideas and then, when my husband draws a picture, I write something to go with it. Though my husband wouldn't call himself an artist, and I wouldn't call myself a writer, we keep going.

Ah! But there's a little more to it. Whenever I think of what we do now, there is a word that always comes to mind and makes my heart jump, so I have to spend a moment calming myself down. The word is *in-yeon* and it means something like a fated meeting, a destined connection.

We were both born in Seoul in 1942, the year of the horse. And entered Seoul National University's College of Education in 1961, where we met. It happened at the beginning of our third year, when there was a poems and paintings exhibition held in our college. I submitted a very short poem entitled "Apple," and another student I had never met before was assigned to illustrate my poem. From the very moment I saw it, I was so pleased with the painting for my poem. It was an abstract painting, and it was perfect for my poem; it made me appreciate anew the words I had written.

Filled with joy, I looked at the student who had painted the picture. It was Chan Jae Lee. On the final day of the exhibition all the participating students celebrated with a popcorn party. And, realizing that our routes home went in the same direction, the two of us ended up walking together.

Who would have thought that the seed of a new *in-yeon* planted in 1963— that poem and complementary painting—which brought us together and grew into our love, would grow new shoots fifty-two years later in 2015, and produce such a lovely bloom as this book in 2020, when we are approaching eighty.

We both lived through the Korean War at the same age and spent our childhoods in poverty before making it to university, so there are many traits and experiences that we share. While Chan Jae was away for three years completing his compulsory military service, I suffered so much that I might as well have gone and served in his place. The rest of the time we were dating, we'd meet almost every day and talk about everything under the sun. I can't remember all the details from back then anymore, but something I can still clearly remember are the students with acoustic guitars sitting on the campus lawn singing "Blowin' in the Wind."

We got married in 1967 when we were just twenty-five. In hindsight, it seems early, but it felt right at the time. We talked about it a lot, and since we were both set on becoming teachers we agreed there was no need for us to have our own children. We started out our married life in a rented room in Singil-dong. It was just a small room in our landlord's home, but it did have its own kitchenette. I can still see that redbrick house vividly in my mind's eye. Both of us worked full time as schoolteachers; my husband taught earth science and I taught Korean. We were happy for a couple of years without having children, but after a while the idea of having our own little people around became more appealing, and early in the morning on March 1, 1971, I gave birth to our first child. Right after our son was born, we bought our most-prized possession, an Asahi Pentax camera, just to take photographs of him. We were a conscientious young couple and adhered to the government slogan of "Regardless if they're girls or boys, have only two and raise them right." Well . . . we weren't really all that conscientious. It's just that was what everyone did back then. You'd encounter that slogan day and night, everywhere you went, and it had a strange persuasive power that you couldn't help but follow.

In the 1970s South Korea was still a very poor country, and in 1974, my parents and younger siblings packed up and emigrated to Brazil in search of a better life. Then in March of the following year, our daughter was born. I cried so much, feeling utterly alone . . . I didn't have any particular reason to be sad, but I cried and cried. Back then there was no word for it so I didn't know, but I think now that I must have had postpartum depression. In the summer of that same year, however, I was excited when we bought a Taihan Electric Wire refrigerator. Those were happy days. As we installed our new refrigerator in the kitchen of our first proper home, we whispered that it was our second most-prized possession, after the camera. We kept rabbits in the yard and there was a wild red rose vine that spread along the wall outside. The dog, Kongkongi, and the goldfish living in the little pond in the garden were our son's friends.

Then one day, my father visited from Brazil. When my parents moved to Brazil with my three younger brothers and sister, they had left behind three daughters, including me, who had already married. But now Father had come back to take the rest of us and our families with him. He met each of his three sons-in-law in turn and asked them if they would go. The three sons-in-law all answered "Yes!" and so he went to see the three sets of parents-in-law, to ask if they would allow their sons and daughters-in-law to go, and their answers were the same. It was 1981 when we got on the plane from Gimpo Airport, without any fear or trepidation.

Thanks to help from my younger siblings, we were able to settle down in São Paulo comfortably enough. Two years later, when we were getting used to life in a new place, we opened up a clothing store called Boutique Symphony. My husband would buy the clothing and our three Brazilian employees and I took care of selling it. That first year, and the next year, too, our sales were so good at Christmas that the kids would come out to the store to help with folding gift boxes, and we had to hire a couple of extra part-timers. Who knew that running a store could be so exciting? It really is true what people in Korea used to say, that being in business is better than being a PhD! Of course, we thought then that the economy would stay that way forever. Not because we were foolish, or couldn't read Brazilian newspapers. Being ordinary, ambitious, and hardworking people—unable to sense that a world of uncertainty, an unpredictable time had arrived—we just lived according to the law of inertia, expecting each day to be like the day before. Even now, Koreans living in Brazil say the same thing every year, "This year was even worse than the last. What can we do?" And then their Brazilian friends comfort them with, "*Vai melhorar*," it'll get better.

The years rolled by and our children had their own children. First, Arthur and Allan, our daughter's two sons born a year apart, were our angels. Sometimes, as I held one of them in my arms, they became my own son, who I would hug that way so long ago back in Seoul. Other times they would become pure softness itself, the likes of which I had never felt before. The love I have for them has been a huge gift to me in my old age. When the children turned three, I felt as though I was turning three, too, and when they entered the first year of elementary school, I was there right with them. We would play hide-and-seek together and a game where we tried to think of as many words starting with the letter "A" as we could. After my husband retired, it became his job to drive Arthur and Allan to school, and he worked hard at the morning and afternoon school run for five years.

The time we spent with our grandchildren was so warm and lovely, but then our daughter suddenly announced that they were moving to Korea. It came as such a shock.

Although he was already living far away in New York, it was our son who was most worried about what would become of his father once our daughter's family left for Korea in January 2015. He knew his father would end

Hand drawn postcard, 1978

up spending all his time staring blankly at the television. One day, out of the blue, our son suggested, "Dad, you should draw." He had remembered how, when he was a boy, his father would draw him pictures on scraps of cardboard. But having grown stubborn over the years, my husband wouldn't listen. "What nonsense! Why would I suddenly start drawing?" But I joined forces with our son to persuade him to take up drawing again. One day he finally got tired of listening to us and drew a cityscape with the caption: "depressing clouds," followed by a horse, a statue, and some random things like lampposts, palm trees, and trash cans. I began to write longer captions for the drawings and then our son taught us how to post them on Instagram so he could keep track of what we were up to. But after a few months, the frequency of drawings diminished as my husband's interest dwindled.

A few months later, our third grandson, Astro, was born in New York! We were overjoyed and we traveled to New York to meet him in person. Over dinner one evening my husband suddenly asked our son, "I wonder what Astro will be when he grows up?"

"Why is that?" our son asked.

"Because, by then, I won't be around anymore."

My son fell quiet for a moment . . . He said later that he had never thought about his parents' old age in that way before, or about what was inevitable someday. Then he had an idea, and suggested to his father that he start drawing for his grandchildren, so that when they were older, they would be able to know what kind of person their grandpa was. We also agreed that when I wrote a little story to go with each picture, our son would translate it into English and our daughter would translate it into Portuguese.

That was how my husband started drawing for our grandchildren.

We called the Instagram account "Drawings_for_My_Grandchildren." Then our son made a very simple video, explaining why and how a grumpy old man more than seventy years old had started using Instagram, and posted it on Facebook. The video resonated with people around the world and quickly spread, getting millions of "likes."

Amazingly enough, since my husband began drawing for our grand-children, even though he usually hates being tied down by anything, he keeps drawing every day. Without anyone pushing him, he also photographs the drawings with his phone and uploads them to Instagram. And he shares them and reads the comments people leave us, all by himself. He takes a lot of pains not to make any mistakes, and although he is quite used to it all now, I know that it really isn't easy for him. It's hard for older people to have confidence when it comes to being creative, not to mention

Drawings from the New York trip

working with technology. After just a day or two without practicing, computers and smartphones can feel so confusing.

Eventually, our son's video caught the attention of a BBC journalist who shared the video along with an article about us. That's how this "Korean grandfather's long-distance Instagram story-telling" became famous. We had a flood of requests for interviews from all sorts of media outlets, and it was really strange and wonderful when former students and school friends started getting in touch after having seen the news. The comments and messages we get from around the world always touch our hearts, even now. Things like,

"Thank you for sharing this with us,"
"This picture is so warm,"
"I'm crying!"
"I miss my grandparents now that they have passed away."

Our two grandsons left Brazil for South Korea not fluent in speaking Korean or reading Hangul, but they enjoyed Korean school life. It was such a surprise to me, and I felt truly thankful . . . They enjoyed their lunches at the school canteen and walked to school together and tried out all sorts of different sports in the park with their new friends. But there was just one thing. "Grandma! Grandpa! When are you coming to join us?"

And so, the two of us returned to Korea in late October 2017, after thirty-six years away. While we were gone, Korea had become a developed country. A wonderful but bewildering country, where the young people are all much taller, and our cell phones beep with warnings to beware of the bad air quality and notifications to check whether our supply of blood pressure medication needs topping up.

One day in August 2019, when we were finally feeling more accustomed to life back in Korea, we jumped for joy when we heard the most wonderful news from New York.

Today we welcomed Lua into the world! Mother and baby are both doing well.

Poring over the photographs our son sent us, we both felt so elated. Just like her name, which means moon in Portuguese, Lua was bright and beautiful. In her face the two of us could see a resemblance to her great-grandma, Chan Jae's mother. And we could also see our son, Ji Byol, and our daughter, Miru. Family resemblance is some wondrous magic!

At the end of January 2020, when we traveled to New York and finally held baby Lua, we just couldn't stop chuckling because Lua kept looking up at us with the biggest smile. What an amazing power she has to make anyone she smiles at happy!

In the beginning, all the drawings were signed "*For AAA*," taking the initials of each of our grandchildren's first names: Arthur, Allan, and Astro. Now that our granddaughter, Lua, has come along, her very proud grandpa has added an "*L*" to the end of his signature, saying to her, "I hope you'll read my heart, too, little one."

Back in Korea again, just like before, we draw pictures and write about them for our grandchildren here and our grandchildren in the United States. Today, just like yesterday, and tomorrow, too, we'll keep drawing pictures and writing, just like this.

—*Grandma Marina with Grandpa Chan*

LOOKING BACK
LIFE WAS BEAUTIFUL

Remember to look up at the stars
and not down at your feet.

—STEPHEN HAWKING

Spring

YOUR EVERY LITTLE THING

Hey, Astro,

Did you know we went to an art gallery with you when you were just around one year old?

I can still remember it vividly, how you ran around taking everything in, your eyes sparkling. You liked the paintings by Henri Rousseau best. Thinking back to that day, I remember that you asked your grandpa to paint you a picture called *Dream*.

What dreams did you dream today, Astro? Could you draw them so we can see them? We're curious about your every little thing.

TIME TRAVEL

As he can't talk yet, little Astro keeps taking Grandpa by the hand and dragging him to his room. When Grandpa beats the drums, Astro dances around. Grandpa with his drumming and Astro with his dancing, both are absorbed in their play.

The minutes go by, and Grandpa's thoughts begin to wander through time. He goes back to when he was three or four. Back into his memories, back to that age, when his father would beat on the door, as if it were a drum—*Tung! Tung!*—and he would dance to that rhythm: *du-doong-doong du doong du-doong-doong-doong.*

Just as the sound of the drum turned Grandpa into his own father, it turned Astro into that father's son, his grandpa, back when he was a boy.

A LOVELY SIGHT

On a rainy day, the two of you are walking together.
Brothers, walking home side by side under the same umbrella.
It might be raining, but there's plenty for you brothers to see.
It warms my heart to watch you two, walking out ahead.

GOULDIAN FINCHES

These days your grandpa and I are finally discovering how full of beauty the world is. When we were younger, we were so busy trying to keep up with everything, we didn't see it. Does this mean we've finally matured? Everything is so mysterious and beautiful. Besides, these days we can see glimpses of the whole world no matter where we are.

Have you ever heard of the Gouldian finch who lives in Australia? They are around four inches tall, and just look at their vibrant colors! Nothing can beat the beauty of nature.

Does that mean we humans are beautiful, too?

CHILDREN HAVE THEIR OWN LANGUAGE

We are on a family outing to the Museum of Natural History.
Astro keeps chattering away, so Arthur and Allan ask him,
"What's that you're saying?"

"T. rex, T. rex . . ." Astro climbs up onto Allan's shoulders
and Arthur puts them both on his shoulders, making a tower.
Astro is a doctor of paleontology! He has so many questions
for that T. rex. Arthur and Allan were just the same at his age,
so without a grumble, they lift Astro up to get a closer look.
But the T. rex's face is still so far away.
Astro keeps muttering on and on, and the T. rex
just smiles. Astro's cousins can't catch what he is saying,
but it seems as if the T. rex understands.

Astro is two years old now.
He still has his own language.
He speaks it endlessly
These words that his cousins don't always understand
But that T. rex understood immediately.

MOMENTS WHEN WE MISS YOU

Out of nowhere, come moments when we want to hear your voices.
At times like this, we draw and write just as we are doing now.

TO ALL THE MOTHERS AND CHILDREN OF THE WORLD

In the photograph Astro is playing with his mom at an indoor
playground. He must have been really happy in that moment.
He loves playing with other people. And it looks like he's having
even more fun because he's with his mom. Even if the child in
the picture wasn't Astro, it would still be a joy to see.
Isn't every child happy when they get to play with their mom?
Just being together is wonderful enough.

Ah! I want to give this picture to all the working mothers in the world.
It doesn't feel like so long ago that I was a working mother, too.
For a large part of my life, I was a working mom. Yes, I'll dedicate
this to all the working moms, always worrying about their children.
And to all the children, too, who feel a little lonely when Mom
is busy working.

ARE WE ANY DIFFERENT?

A dog is crying. Can you guess why?

Anyone who's had a dog as part of their family knows that dogs have their own joys and sorrows. One moment they are feeling a little lonely when no one is home, the next they are full of joy at the sight of their humans walking in the door. There's a story behind why the dog in the picture couldn't help but cry.

An animal protection group raised money to rescue dogs from a dog farm in Kunming in China. They managed to save twenty. One of those dogs started crying when the person who saved him stroked his head. What joy the dog must have felt. That feeling of safety after being in such an uncertain situation must have been overwhelming.
I try to imagine the dog's emotions in that moment.
Are we humans really any different than this dog crying with gratitude to the person who saved his life?

SPRING APPROACHES AND THEN IT'S GONE

Spring is arriving in São Paulo, but in Seoul and New York
autumn must be on its way out. Seasons come and go around the world;
sometimes they hang about for a while, other times they just roll on
through. People who know spring in São Paulo know that often
just when it seems it's on its way, it's over.

WHEN THE TIME COMES

Astro's gazing out of the window.
He stands there for a really long time.
That image of him from behind conveys so much.
He's looking down at the street below the window
waiting for Grandma and Grandpa, who played with him
all day long, to reappear.
He thinks back to when Grandma and Grandpa drove off in a car.
That image of Astro from behind, all alone, makes my heart ache.

You know what, Astro? Although you won't recognize it yet,
that thing which has left a little, tiny mark on your heart,
is the pain called parting.

That pain will soon turn into longing, into missing someone.

I hope that someday, when the time comes and you experience
such pain again, you'll know by then that there's also the joy
of being reunited.

DOCTOR GRANDPA

It happened the other morning.

"Hey, Astro, get over here. Did you sleep well?" Astro came over to his grandpa but didn't respond.

"What's wrong? Are you hurt? Astro?" Astro didn't say anything. He climbed up onto Grandpa's bed and pointed at his lip. He must have hit it against something.

"Oh no! That must be painful. Hey, Astro, if Grandpa blows on it, it won't hurt anymore."

With one shot of breath from Grandpa, Astro brightened right up and pulled at Grandpa's hand. Grandpa knew that this meant he must want him to go to his room to play. And so Grandpa and Astro played together in Astro's room all day long.

A CHILD'S FEET

Children grow.
A little each hour,
a little each day
they keep growing.

SOMEONE'S SON, SOMEONE'S FATHER

I was walking along the street one day when I saw a man in his forties at a stall, sharpening a knife. Turning the wheel with his feet, holding the knife in both hands, and singing a song as he worked, he was happily focused on doing what he does well. I went over to him and asked how many knives he sharpens a day. He gave a broad smile as he answered, "Eight to ten." I didn't have the heart to ask how much he gets paid for each one.

He must be someone's son, and probably someone's father, too. In Brazil, the second Sunday of August is Father's Day. A day when fathers get a special hug. Although every good father deserves so much more, even with that, a father's face will light up in a smile . . .

BUTTERFLIES

See all those butterflies flying around? It's such a beautiful sight.
Looking at this bright blur of lustrous color and movement,
I suddenly remembered an old song we used to sing when I was a child.

Hey, butterfly, let's go to the lush mountain.
Hey, swallowtail, you come along, too.
If it gets dark as we make our way, let's stop for the night in a flower.
If we're not welcomed in the flower we can always just sleep on a leaf.

That earnest wish, to fly together, spiraling upward,
to a lush green mountain—it seems people in the olden days
wanted to escape the human world sometimes, too.
Why might they have felt that way back then?

I remember how I used to run and jump about all summer trying
to catch butterflies.
It was our vacation assignment. In Korea, the most common were
cloudless sulfurs and cabbage whites.
If I happened to spot a tiger swallowtail my heart would pound
with excitement.
You can imagine how amazed I was when I got to Brazil and saw
my first blue butterfly.

TIME REALLY DOES GO BY
BEFORE YOU KNOW IT

There are times when your grandma forgets we're living in Brazil.
Especially when I'm looking up at clouds floating by in the sky.
It's been thirty-five years since we moved here from Korea.
Like those clouds floating past in the wide-open sky,
time went by and had passed before I knew it.
That man walking alone by that water is floating away like a cloud, too.

WHAT WAS IT LIKE AGAIN?

Astro is kicking a ball with his dad. He's running excitedly on soft
grass. Playing soccer with Dad looks like so much fun. *"Ah ha ha ha!"*
Astro's laughter makes the trees and flowers smile brightly.

That sound echoing out of the yard must make the neighbors say,
"Astro's playing a soccer match with his dad! Shall we join in?"

Astro's dad is a really good soccer coach.
I think back to when Astro's dad was a boy. What was it like again?
I can't remember whether my husband played soccer with our son.
He probably just laid down and watched baseball on television,
complaining about how tired he was.

TEACHER, TEACHER!

A group of children are sitting on the grass in a circle, listening to
their teacher. What a lovely sight to come across as I'm out walking.
To me they are all just like our Astro and our Allan. I wonder what they
are learning as they sit in this little circle? I slow down to watch them.

There's a child watching ants.
A child picking the little flowers in the grass,
a child looking intently at the teacher, no matter how much their
neighbor pokes them . . .

I feel like going over to join them. I want to put my hand up and ask
a question, too. "Teacher, teacher! Who would win if a tiger and a lion
had a fight?" No, no. That's the kind of question people might have
asked long ago, when tigers could talk; no one would be curious about
that sort of thing now.

"Teacher, teacher! Who do you like better, Spider-Man or Iron Man?"

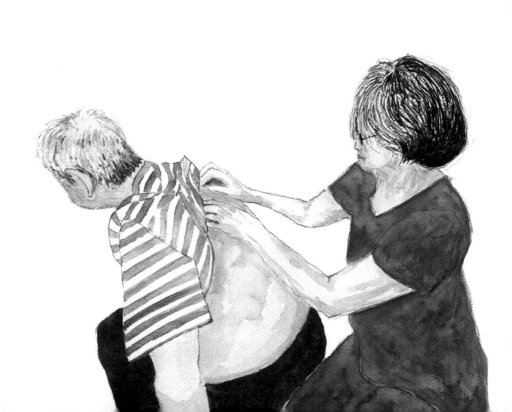

ITCHING BACK

Why does your back get so itchy when you get old?
You don't get an itchy belly or chest . . . At least once a day Grandpa
will shout out of nowhere: "Please! Scratch me!" I know how he feels.
How urgent it is. I'm in the same situation. So I rush over, lift his shirt,
and start scratching.

"Up a bit, down a bit, to the left . . . no to the right a bit,
a little lower . . . Oh! Right there!" I can always find it.
Exactly where the itch is coming from!

I've long since given up on growing my nails or putting on nail polish.
I need to be able to scratch hard. But no matter how diligently I scratch,
it's never fully satisfying. Perhaps because it's no use anyway,
or because he feels bad for me, after a while Grandpa will say,
"Alright, that's enough!"

A SMALL COMFORT

It's still early morning! Tiny streams of sunlight peek through the branches of the trees. There are three men sitting on a bench beside one of the busiest paths in the park where many people come and go. I can't tell if they've come here together, whether they're friends or else just strangers. The man in a stylish black hat sings as he plays the guitar, and for some reason I feel sadness coming from the two men beside him. Although it may not be much, I hope the soft, sweet bossa nova melody will be some comfort to them on a difficult day.

THE DINOSAUR MAGIC TRICK

This picture of a dinosaur was painted in deep blue. It's a T. rex.
The color seems to make the dinosaur even more mysterious.
I'll tell you the story of how this picture came to be.

A young mother sent your grandpa an invitation.
"Please come and visit my son's preschool. The children would love it if
you came and talked to them about drawing and also Korean culture."

What could we do? The two of us thought it over for a long time.
Then we had the perfect idea and, of course, it involved dinosaurs.
We had heard that Astro, also in preschool, loves dinosaur books these
days. Grandpa drew a whole load of dinosaurs and took them with him.
As soon as he showed the four- and five-year-old children the dinosaur
pictures, their eyes all lit up.

"Do you want to try drawing one, too?"

They began to draw, deep in concentration. They'd been so noisy
just moments before, but the children were totally silent in no time.
Why do young children love dinosaurs so much?

RUNNING

Astro is running.
He runs with bare feet, but he's really fast.
I don't know what's so funny, but he bursts out laughing.
He runs well, without falling over.
Is running that much fun?

The trees applaud,
and the girl who lives next door shouts,
"Faster! Faaaasteeer!"

It's just the two of us who are a little anxious.
That's enough now Astro, stop! Astro!

GRANDMA'S LEARNING, EVEN NOW

At three and a half years old, Astro has started school.
Apparently, he wailed and clung to his mom by the gate every day
for the first week, but from the third week on he's been going in smiling.
That's our Astro! Congratulations! Just as you went rock climbing
and crossed a rope bridge and enjoyed every minute of your vacation in
Seoul, you'll make the most of your days at school now, too, won't you?

But going to school at such a young age . . .
I don't know whether it's a good thing or a bad thing.
There is still so much your grandma doesn't know.

ALL THE THINGS IN THE WORLD

A cart piled high with loads of different things is stopped on a busy
street. I was reminded of the days before we had plastic, when trays and
mats were woven out of bamboo or straw. And I thought of the women
who would balance massive bundles of baskets, large and small, on their
heads, and walk around to sell them. It might look like junk, but each
and every item there is something we could use as we live our lives.

I want to help the seller make a sale. There it is.
In among all that stuff, I've seen something I really need.
I'll just have to buy it.

MOTHER, MY MOTHER

I have no memory of ever giving my mother flowers.
But I can still sing that song by heart, the one we sing in Korea
on Parents' Day, to the very end, or to the second verse at least . . .

They say that there are vast things beneath the sky,
but nothing is greater than a mother's sacrifice.

Now and then, when I can't remember something, I think to myself,
I'll have to ask Mom, but soon I realize she passed away a long time ago,
and the thought makes me so sad all over again. I did wrong by my
mother so many times, and now I can't even remember why.

I really miss you, Mom.

SUNSET

I'm trying to work out what the focus of this picture is.
Could it be the sun? The island? The sea?
Or else that one bird?
Whichever way I look at it, I think it must be that rich red.

The sun goes down.
In the end, it'll sneak down below the horizon.
An old man has traveled a long way just to capture this moment.
He takes his camera to faraway places, even in springtime,
just to get a few great shots.
Every time I see a sunset my heart leaps.

A FRIEND HAS LEFT US

"A good friend has passed away," my husband said.
Stephen Hawking, born in 1942.
Although they never met, he was the same age as your grandpa.
And they were both fascinated by space, so I know Grandpa
considered him a kindred spirit. People say that the ways of the world
are so strange you could never believe them, but Professor Hawking
confronted the mysteries of the universe—one man with one mind.
He showed us what human greatness can be.
Our teacher can travel freely now,
from this star to that in the endless spread of stars.
Let's make a special place for him deep in our hearts,
and repeat again and again the message he left us:
"Remember to look up at the stars and not down at your feet."

TIMES GONE BY

I noticed an elderly woman on the subway into the city.
A grandma in the seats for the elderly or infirm, she sat very upright
and straight, staring over at the seats for younger people.
I could sense the feeling of loneliness in her.
Where could she be going on a day when the dust is bad,
wearing a mask with her walking stick in hand? I wondered about
the grandma's younger years, about her youthful days gone by.

THE LAST RHINO

I read an article about the death of Sudan, the last male northern white rhino, who lived on a plain in Kenya. We hear all the time about animals being endangered, but he was the very last one of his kind! In the picture, he stood, heavy and strong, with a forceful expression. And I thought I could hear him crying out to us:

"Do you still think there's a future for you, too?"

A SCENE I COULD NEVER HAVE IMAGINED

The cold is retreating.
The weather is still chilly,
but in my mind its spring already, that's how impatient I am.
You could say it's a fickle luxury,
unique to those of us who enjoy four distinct seasons.

There are many more people riding bikes by the river now.
I don't know how to ride a bike myself, so I can only watch jealously
from afar. But there's a problem: all the fine dust in the air.

The buildings in the distance are barely visible, and even the water in
the river has turned grey-white, reflecting the sky. When I was a girl,
I could never even have imagined that people would have to wear
air-filter masks when they went cycling. Yesterday we even received
a warning to refrain from going outside.

THE RAIN IS WELCOME TODAY

It's May, queen of the seasons.
The time when all the leaves change from a pretty pea green
to a deep green.
A welcome rain has been falling since the morning.
The road to school is full of children walking happily under
their umbrellas.
The leaves are happy, too, as the rain has washed all the dust away.

YOUR OWN WORLD

Hey, Astro,

When you were five months old, you'd babble all day long.
You communicated with all your might, with your arms and legs, too,
wriggling in the air. Even though your grandma is so far away,
I thought I could hear you. Thoughts and stories all your own grow
in number day by day. A whole world belonging to Astro,
that no one else can see.

WALKING TOGETHER

You probably noticed that your grandma and grandpa often quarrel,
right? But something has changed lately. Grandpa used to really hate it
when two or three people were walking slowly side by side.
He always thought that people walking like that are a nuisance
and get in everyone else's way, so he would never walk beside me
and was always striding out ahead.
He wouldn't even look around to see whether I was following.
But now that we are back in Korea and often have to take the subway,
it is so very crowded in the stations and it's hard for me to get up and
down the stairs, so I get really anxious. One day I started holding on to
Grandpa's arm, and we ended up walking arm in arm again.
It's wonderful. It brings back happy memories, too.

Well, a few nights ago we took a stroll together, the May breeze
blowing so nicely, and out of nowhere Grandpa took my hand and even
entwined our fingers. Since then there haven't been any quarrels.

PEACEFUL

A child is fast asleep.
Quietly, carefully, I gaze upon the child's face.
The child is cradled in peace.

*In 2017, Grandpa was invited by
National Geographic to travel to
the Galápagos Islands on a ten-day
expedition and draw his experience.
The drawings were published in
an article in the magazine.*

Galápagos

VIVID COLORS

Among all the animals I saw in the Galápagos Islands,
my favorite was the blue-footed booby bird. Do you know how
its feet get to be such a dazzling turquoise?
It's because of the fish the birds eat. The bluer their feet,
the healthier they are, and that's why female booby birds go
in search of mates with the bluest feet.

Your grandpa hopes that, just like the blue-footed booby bird,
each of you will grow up to have your own vivid color.

WHAT HAPPENED

When a male frigate bird is trying to attract a mate,
he inflates the huge red pouch in his throat and makes a really
loud drumming sound.
Do you think it's only animals that do that? Not a chance!
When your grandpa was at university, I'd make myself look
as cool as I could, and then go around singing pop songs.
And would you believe it?
A nice young lady started to take an interest in me.
That's how we fell in love.

WHAT THE ANIMALS SAID

The tortoise ambling along, slow and steady,
stuck his head up toward me and said,
"All those years gone by, I bet you feel like they were just an instant now."

You'll never believe it, but without even turning to look at me
as I approached her, a sea lion lounging on the shore said,
"What are you so curious about?"

It was only by coming here that your grandpa learned how awful
we humans are. How foolish we are, how ignorant we are of what
the not too distant future could hold! How dare we make this world,
the world where we live, the world that our children and their children
will inhabit, face such danger . . .

Every day, a new adventure . . .

This giant turtle is much older than Grandpa.

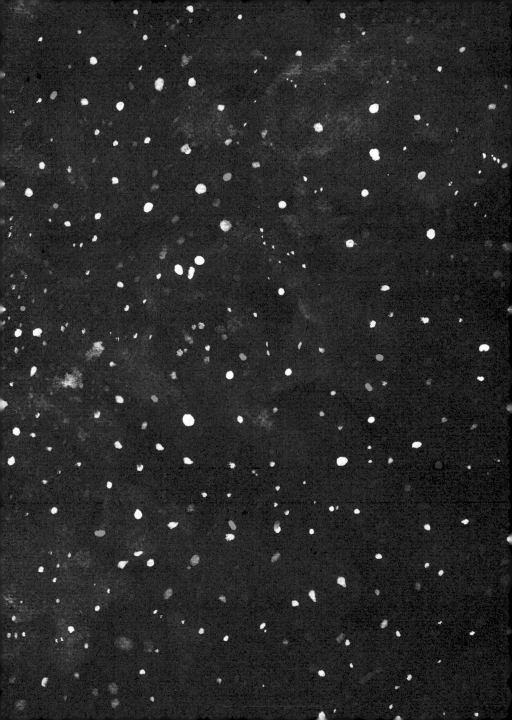

THE NIGHT SKY

The other evening your grandpa suddenly became sad looking up
at the night sky. I was remembering how, as a child, every evening I
would gaze up at the night sky and ask the grown-ups to tell me the
names of the constellations and the mythical stories surrounding them.
One star, two stars, three . . . I would fall asleep counting stars sprawled
out on a bamboo mat my mother had laid out in the front yard.

When did I stop looking at the sky?
I mean, the sky has been above me every day and every night of my life.

That evening we were in the Galápagos Islands and seeing the stars
taught me something. Your grandpa started looking back over his life.
For so many years, I thought life was just a constant stream of difficulty,
distress, and exhaustion, but when I look back now, I can see that life
was beautiful. Your grandpa didn't realize it for so long,
but the stars that evening taught me.

TO MY A, A, A, AND L

Astro, a one-of-a-kind shining star.
Upright, honest Arthur, and ever-curious Allan.
Baby Lua, who has just joined our family.
Lua, who I can't wait to give a big hug.
I won't be around anymore when you're all grown up
and think of me from time to time,
but I'm writing letters and drawing pictures now for you then.
If you come to this place when you're older, I'm sure that,
just like me, you'll feel deep in your heart how precious life is.
Although it's such a fragile thing,
life's unpredictability is what makes it so magical.

Nature whispers to me softly.
Look at the sky.
Look at the stars.
Notice the curves of cacti.
See the feathers of a white bird.
Look out to that rocky island.
Watch as the sun sets.
Listen to the seagulls' song.
Hear the sound of the waves.

Children grow even faster in summer.

Summer

CHILDREN GROW EVEN FASTER IN SUMMER

Seeing the insect Grandpa painted on a rock, Astro said, "It's a ladybug!"
I could hardly believe my ears.
Grandpa was so excited, he drew a picture of a flower bed with
many such friends hidden here and there and we played at finding all
the little creatures in the picture.

Summer, the season of insects, is passing by.
It's not just bees and butterflies,
on a hot summer day, you'll find our Astro, too, flittering around
all over the place.
Children grow even faster in summer.
Like ripening grapes, they get big and sweet.

PLAYING IN THE WATER

On a scorching summer day, you all came with me to visit
my friend's house.
You splashed around in the swimming pool
and lay down for a while to rest in the shade
and got into a small tub and laughed and played games.
Playing in the water, we all forgot it was very, very hot.

TROUBLED WORLD

The whole sky is grey.
A thin rain is coming down, so hardly anyone is going by outside.
The house is too quiet, I think I will put on some cheerful music.

It's not often you see anything positive in the news these days.
I feel anxious, worrying that something bad could happen
in the world, kicked off by the slightest provocation.
The number of uncaring people seems to grow day by day.

Staring out at the sky, I find I'm praying in spite of myself,
praying for peace in your future.
I think I will ask your grandpa to paint a rainbow of hope for you.

BICYCLE IN THE FOREST

Look, there's a bicycle resting in the forest, propped up against a tree.
Someone must have left it there. Perhaps they decided to rest here
a moment since the flowers are so beautiful and the air so clear?

It's your mom, Astro. You know, don't you?
Not long ago, your mom was sick. She's all better now.
She doesn't even need to take medicine anymore and she can ride
her bicycle and cycle to places like this.
She said that when she was finally well enough to visit the seaside,
just twenty miles from home, she felt overwhelmed with emotion.

So, let's look at the picture again.
There are so many stories in it, don't you think?

HE'S BECOME ONE WITH THE TREE

Allan climbs up into a tree.

On his way up, he stops for a moment to catch his breath.

As soon as his mom spots him like that, she shouts,

"Don't climb so high, Allan!"

Allan doesn't respond.

"Didn't I already tell you? You'll fall!"

Allan wraps himself around the tree and stays perfectly still.

When I turn back to look again, Allan is gone; all I can see is that
the tree trunk has grown thicker all of a sudden.

Oh my! Allan's become a tree.

I JUST LOOKED ON

On the first day of our exhibition, a man came into the gallery
tapping a long, thin stick on the ground in front of him.
He had a helper, too, who walked alongside him.
"They can't have come to see the pictures, surely?"

But my commonsense thinking was too common that day. I was wrong.
They stopped and stood in front of each picture. I can't even tell you
how nervous I felt as I watched them. The helper would stop in front of
a picture and describe its every detail. After she had spoken for a while,
they would move along to the next one. They both looked very content.

I wanted to stand nearby and listen, but I thought I should be careful
not to disturb them, so I just looked on from across the gallery.
I looked on with my heart trembling.

Can you imagine what the pictures might have looked like
in that man's mind?

ASTRO ON HIS SCOOTER

Watching a video of Astro speeding on his scooter like a pro,
I was reminded of one bright, early Brooklyn morning when he
was four months old.

I woke up early, so I put little Astro in his stroller and took him out.
The streets were quiet and even the wind was still, but when we got
to the park it was already busy welcoming children. There was one
child who caught my eye that day; he must have been around two.
He was only a toddler, but he was racing around on a scooter without
any help! *Goodness me!* I thought. I didn't even know that was possible.
Will our Astro be able to ride like that someday, too?
I was so amazed by that little boy, and wondered if someday
Astro would be as good at scootering as he was.

Astro, having grown so much in no time, races around just as well as
that child did. Now there will be someone, some grandma just like me,
looking at you and looking forward to when her grandchild will be able
to race around like you, too. Who knows what more Astro will be able
to do five years from now? Don't forget that we're always watching,
eager to see what you do next.

GRANDPA'S SHORTS

What do you think of Grandpa in shorts?
Don't you think he looks great? They take years off him!
He went like this to his high school alumni reunion.
It was a meeting of elderly people, all nearly eighty.
They gathered at a restaurant in the afternoon, and had a nice time
talking about this and that for a couple of hours.
As it was very hot, without thinking too much,
Grandpa dressed in denim shorts, just like he used to do in Brazil.
But it seems that in Korean society, wearing such casual clothing
reflects a lack respect for such an occasion.
Apparently one of Grandpa's close friends approached him quietly
and gave him a light warning not to come in shorts next time.
Grandpa nodded yes without any reluctance.
There's no reason he has to go out in shorts.

RELAY RACE

Even just thinking about a relay race makes me nervous.
What if I fail to grab hold of the baton?
Or what if I can't pass it on properly?
What if I drop the baton, or else can't run fast enough?
Or . . . oh no! What if I fall over?

I imagined you boys having a relay race of your own.
The baton was a bunch of flowers. Arthur passed the flowers to Allan,
and Allan passed them to Astro.

Astro wanted to give the flowers to his favorite baby dinosaur.
Will his friend take them? We all knew that the flowers were actually
just love, so we were pretty sure he'd accept them gladly.

The baby dinosaur runs, and at last . . . ! Oh, that's funny . . .
The dinosaur turned around and gave the flowers back to Astro.

The relay started all over again.

ARTHUR'S FIRST SHAVE

Arthur, when I saw the photo of you doing your first shave
at age fourteen, I felt so proud. Do you know why?
Maybe because you're no longer a boy: You're a man now.
I asked your grandpa when he first started shaving,
but he said he couldn't remember.

I had noticed that you were looking a bit scruffy lately.
Was it your mom who suggested you do it? Did you feel fresh?
Did it go well? It can't have been all that easy.
But now that you've started shaving, you'll have to become an expert!

TROPICAL FISH

Arthur will be attending middle school soon. I'm so proud.
The two brothers who went straight into school as soon as they arrived
in Korea, even though they couldn't speak or read Korean well, have
now completed the fifth and sixth grades. They both did very well.
I kept thinking about what would make a good gift to congratulate you,
Arthur, and then I finally had an idea. I remembered how you kept
two little fish in a fish tank when you lived in Brazil,
so I asked Grandpa to draw you some pretty fish.

To tell the truth, I had another reason, too. I'd always hoped that when
you got to middle school you would read "The Gift of Understanding"
by American writer Paul Villiard. Every time I taught that story in class
I would tear up. I always hoped that I could write something like that
myself one day. The story has tropical fish in it.

ASTRO DANCING

Astro, you are turning three before the end of April.
The sight of you dancing is so amazing to me.
The way you move is just like a traditional Korean dancer.
How did you get to know the old Korean rhythm and energy?
Did you see it somewhere? Or learn it?
Or did you discover that beat and way of moving all by yourself?
Watching you dance I can tell that there are Korean genes
flowing through you.

COUPLES

Arthur, when Grandma was in the third year of middle school, like you are now, I went to a secret reading club that my school seniors had made. There were boys there, too. It was great. We would read things like "Enoch Arden" and "The Lake Isle of Innisfree" together and then have discussions. Around that time there were sometimes boys who would walk me home and give letters to my friends to pass on to me. It was a bit scary because I was always worried my father would find out. Even when I was at university and was courting with your grandpa, when we got close to my home I'd start to worry in case someone saw us walking side by side.

Returning to Korea after thirty-six years, I see young couples stealing brief kisses on the street or in the subway. Time has passed and Korea has changed. To your grandma and grandpa, now old and grey, the sight of a young couple sitting close together on a bench is beautiful.

Do you have feelings for anyone, Arthur?

HIDE-AND-SEEK

Our Astro is hiding behind a tree.
"Huh? Where did he go?" I say, as if I am just talking to myself
but loudly enough that I know he will hear. Pretending as if
I don't know exactly where he is, I walk off in the opposite direction,
but Astro knows that he will soon hear his grandma's footsteps again,
so he tries to stay perfectly still, flinching with anticipation.

I don't have any memories of playing hide-and-seek like this with
my mother. She would always have been exhausted, giving birth to
one child after another and trying to raise them, and back then there
was no culture of playing with children. What's more, among seven
siblings I was the second daughter, and from a young age I was always
weak, so there was no way I'd be allowed outside to play with the other
children in the neighborhood. And as for when I was raising my own
children . . . well! I can't even remember what it was like anymore!

Arthur, Allan, do you remember playing hide-and-seek with me?
Now, in no time at all, Astro's at that age. Can't you hear Astro behind
that tree trying to keep his breathing quiet? "Huu huu, huu huu . . ."

After pretending to look here, there, and everywhere for him,
finally I shout, "Oh! There he is! I can see Astro's hair sticking out."
Then I can feel my tummy drop right along with Astro's tummy
as he suddenly realizes that he has been found.

112

THE DEATH OF 416 WHALES

Today I heard something sad and hard to believe. It was the story
of hundreds of whales that died together. Apparently the 416 whales
suddenly washed up onto a sandy beach on the coast of New Zealand.
Strangely, they washed up on the beach in two separate groups of
around two hundred each. People did all they could to save even one
of them; they tried all different kinds of things to get them back into
the ocean. Didn't they want to live?

A while ago I read an article that detailed all of the different kinds
of human trash that was found inside the stomach of a whale in the
North Atlantic. Do you think perhaps those whales in New Zealand
were trying to protest something to humans with their death?
My heart has been heavy all day long. I keep thinking of all the children
who love whales and would not want them to suffer so . . .

PLAYING IN THE SAND

A child is playing in the sand at the river shore.
He sits quietly for a long time, kneading the sand with his hands.
Here's a question for you:
What is the child thinking about?

116

ALL DAY LONG THE CICADAS CRY

Magpies in the morning and cicadas in the daytime.
Listening to their sounds, I forget that we're in the heart of a big city.
In this place, where blocks are packed together tighter than trees
in a forest, the cicadas cry all day long in a roaring chorus.

The cicadas today sound different from times gone by.
Their singing used to be leisurely. They would sing for a while
and then stop, as though deciding to rest, to save their voices.
These days, the cicadas cry together all day long, never stopping.

A question enters my mind. Before all these apartments were built,
would this place have been filled with trees?
In that case, it would have been the cicadas' neighborhood, too.

TILIKUM THE ORCA

A two-year-old orca playing without a care with his family in the cold
and clear North Atlantic Ocean was caught by a hunter.
Out of nowhere, he was given the name of Tilikum, and had to live
a life completely different than before. He had to train all day every
single day, so that he could give us humans an entertaining show.

After much work, the orca became the ultimate performer.
He received endless cheers and applause from the people who came
from all over the world to see him. Tilikum spent thirty whole years
jumping out of the water, twirling high up in the air, then flopping
down with a splash. He was all over the news when he caused one of his
trainers to drown, and he became the focus of a documentary film, too.
Everyone was arguing about whether Tilikum was too dangerous
for humans to work with, and whether it was right for orcas to be
kept in captivity, but no one could even begin to understand the
pent-up anger in his heart. But not long after the incident,
Tilikum was called back out to the orca show pool to perform.

Time passed, and Tilikum got old and fell sick. He suffered for
a year before his life came to a close after thirty-five years.
It was only after he died that Tilikum the orca, who was ten meters
in length, and weighed six tons, was free to return to his ocean
home, the place he must have longed and yearned for.
Now, in the cold, clear ocean, his spirit will be telling all the other
orcas about the meaning of freedom and how precious family
companionship is. I think I can almost hear it.

120

EVENING IN AN ORDINARY NEIGHBORHOOD

An ordinary neighborhood in São Paulo, all the more inviting because it's not a rich one. A neighborhood with red-tiled roofs, white walls, and even the occasional old slate roof, too. The kind of neighborhood that has mature trees and colorful graffiti on the walls.

It's around six in the evening, and I can just picture all the mothers who must be making dinner in their homes. Do you know how hearty the smell of boiling *feijão* is? It smells like someone must be frying chicken wings, too. With all the lovely aromas wafting around, I start to get hungry.

The time when family members return home one by one.
The time when the day comes to a close.
A dinner table made cheerful with stories of the day.
What kind of day did you have today?

PEOPLE IN BRAZIL LOVE GARLIC, TOO!

Today I saw a garlic merchant outside our apartment building.
For some reason, I felt like I'd bumped into an old friend. He felt so
familiar that I followed behind him for quite a while. When he passed
by the corner store, he lifted his bundle of garlic as though it weighed
nothing and shouted out, "Take a look at this garlic. The garlic is here."

That moment, I thought back to our early days after arriving here.
We were driving along a stream near the central market district
and I happened to see a garlic market. That's right, a whole market
just for garlic! Heaps of garlic were piled high like mountains;
there were sacks of garlic and braided garlic stalks studded with bulbs.
What really amazed me was that the braids of garlic were tied together
in exactly the same way as in Korea . . . "Wow, I can't believe it!"

Who knew that people in Brazil would eat so much garlic?
Just that one fact made me think that our life here would turn out
alright. It was only much later that I got a real shock when I heard
that people in Brazil even add garlic when they cook rice.

THE WAYS OF NATURE

This is Jaraguá mountain, seen from our apartment.
We call it Namsan, "south mountain" in Korean.
Doesn't it remind you of Mount Namsan in Seoul?
I look out at it for ages, feeling connected to it somehow,
as though seeing my hometown.

But little by little, dark clouds gather and then,
in less than a minute, it starts to rain really hard.
I'm reminded again that nature is incredibly powerful.

MAKING ITS OWN BEAUTY

Our dear Arthur and Allan, it's already been seven months
since you left. Back when you lived in São Paulo you would inspect
all my houseplants every time you came over. You would examine
the green chilis growing on the chili plant. Once when you had been
away on holiday, the moment you returned you ran to the veranda to
check on my plants. While you were away, the green chilis had turned
a deep red. Look at the beautiful red color of the chili peppers growing
on my plant now, a beauty that the plant made all by itself.

TINY GARDEN

My favorite place in the small apartment we lived in in Brazil was the indoor veranda. We put up blue tiles on the walls and they made the space wonderful. Just that was plenty beautiful already, but I thought, *How about we get a green trailing plant to grow here?* So I hurried to the garden market and bought some long rectangular terra-cotta pots and we hung them on the walls on either side. It looked even better than I'd imagined. The first thing we planted were a few threads of a String of Hearts plant.

In the beginning, I felt a little trapped when I opened the window and saw nothing but the grey buildings of São Paulo, but I was fine once I had my tiny garden, where I planted and cared for each and every thing.

TIGER

July 29 is International Tiger Day. It was established to help save tigers from extinction. Did you know that tigers used to roam all over the Korean Peninsula? People thought they were magical, but they were dangerous, too, and around one hundred years ago overenthusiastic hunters killed the last few off. But the proud tiger returned to Korea in the form of the 1988 Seoul Summer Olympics mascot.

GROWING ALL THE TIME

When we saw Astro again after nine months, his body had grown, of course, but his speaking and his manners and his thoughts had grown so much, too. Some moments I'm taken aback by the words he's suddenly using. But he still has that same special baby energy: never staying still and, though small, strong enough to move the whole family according to his will. It's incredible, really, and enviable.

Astro gets us all up on our feet. "Let's play the train game." He watches to see who plays along with gusto and who isn't making the effort. And he provides those who need it with a little encouragement, so that no one can say "That's enough playing for now." Goodness! We're exhausted. This is hard work!

A THOUGHT I HAD IN THE MOUNTAINS

This mountain is so big and so deep.
How small and shallow we humans are.

ASTRO AND LUA

Astro is looking at the baby.
He strokes her cheek, very carefully.
He quickly pulls back his hand.
The baby moved!

He places his hand on the baby's feet, barely touching.
It's soft! There's nothing softer.

Astro, let the baby sleep. She's still so small!
Don't pester your little sister.
Soon enough she'll be following you around asking endless questions,
What's this, Astro?
Astro, does it hurt a lot?
Why can't I come with you?
Enjoy the quiet now; in no time she'll be bugging you nonstop.

BABY'S CRIB

Astro is quiet. Where is he?

Oh! He's lying in the baby's crib?! Oh dear, it looks like he's been crying. Are you feeling lonely, Astro? I think I know how you feel.

Do you sometimes wish you could be a baby again, too? That's alright. Lay down there for a while. Lay on your side curled up like a baby. The baby smell in the crib will soon send you to sleep. And once you have rested awhile, you'll wake up feeling better. Then you can run over and investigate what the baby is up to, and carefully touch her tiny hands and feet, murmuring, "Lua, my cute little sister, Lua!"

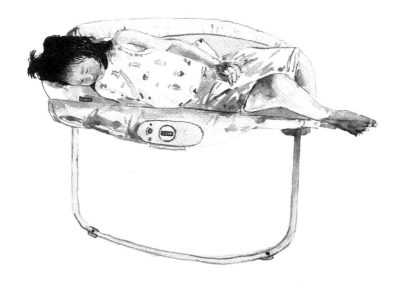

THE PENGUIN WHO RETURNS EVERY YEAR

An old man called João Pereira de Souza lives on an island called
Ilha Grande, near Rio di Janerio. One day, he found a penguin right
outside his home on the verge of death. It was totally soaked with oil.
"Oh dear, you poor thing! What on earth happened?" João started to
clean off the oil with great care. He washed the penguin and fed him,
and at last the four-year-old penguin was healthy again.
But even though João tried to send the penguin back out into the wild,
the little guy just wouldn't go. So he lived with João for a while,
and then one day he finally left. But amazingly enough, the penguin,
who João had named "Dindim," came back again four months later.

Since then, Dindim comes back to João every year and stays with him
for a few months at a time. I'm certain this penguin, Dindim, can
understand Portuguese, and he's so good at showing his gratitude.
Isn't it amazing?

ALL BABIES ARE ANGELS

A young mother is walking down the street carrying her baby.
It looks like the baby is no more than a few months old.
There's so much all around for it to look at that its big glittering eyes
turn this way and that. Everything must be so new and intriguing.
The baby looks exactly like a cherub from a painting by Raphael.
While I walked behind them the baby made eye contact with me,
so I waved. Before I knew it, I was making sounds and silly faces
and the baby was wriggling with glee. I walked like that for a long time.
As soon as I got home, I asked Grandpa to draw it for me:
a baby like an angel.

Grandpa Memories

NIGHT SKY TRUMPET

There are so many melodies from days gone by kept deep in your
grandpa's heart. Thirty years from now, even sixty years from now,
you'll find yourselves humming the songs of the musicians you love so
much today. No matter how much time passes, there's one performance
I can never forget. I heard it on a moonlit night, when your mother
and uncle were only little. It came from the small mountain
beside our old place in Hwagok-dong.

Late at night, when everyone else was fast asleep,
I heard the sound of a trumpet coming from the mountain.
It passed through the trees and spread far and wide, down to
the neighborhood below the mountain, and up into the night sky.
Up into the sky lit up by the beaming moon . . . It was a painfully
beautiful song. I don't know who was playing that trumpet,
but their performance was as beautiful as it was sad.
I held my breath to hear every note.

THE DAY OF MY FIRST ENTRANCE EXAM

Today I'll tell you the story of the first entrance exam I ever took.
Sixty years ago, if you wanted to progress to middle school,
you had to sit for an exam. I was really confident with math back then—
people even called me Dr. Arithmetic—but I got stuck on the very first
question on the test. I just couldn't solve the equation. My chest
tightened. I looked at it again, closely, but I couldn't think of how I
should solve it. The clock kept ticking and I started to sweat profusely.
How could there be a math problem I couldn't solve? How could I get
stuck on such a basic problem! My eyes became so soaked with sweat
and tears that I couldn't even see the numbers anymore.

So, what should you do at times like that? Of course, the sensible thing
to do would be to just move on to the next question. But I stayed totally
stuck, obsessed with needing to solve that first equation, and that meant
I messed up the whole exam. In the end, I didn't get into that middle
school. Kids, try not to be as foolish as your grandpa.

OUR HISTORY IN THE MAKING

It must have been 1963. A friend contacted me to say that our
university literature society was going to hold an exhibition of
poems with pictures, and asked if I would take care of the illustrations.
A young woman gave me her poem and asked me to draw something
for it. It was a short poem titled "Apple." I'm not sure whether it
was the poem or the poet that touched my heart more,
but I drew an illustration and she seemed pleased with it.
On the closing day of the successful exhibition,
everyone got together and had a popcorn party to celebrate.

Who do you think that young woman was?
That's right, kids, that's how our history started.

I REALLY LIKED THAT

It was the summer of 1981 when we arrived in São Paulo.
I think back now on what I was like then: forty years old and not
knowing a single word of Portuguese, the father of two children:
a ten-year-old son and a six-year-old daughter. I must have been
full of apprehension. So much I couldn't put it into words.
But you know what? I don't have any memories of that at all.

Now, I remember a time not long after we arrived,
when I found out that there were markets in each neighborhood
that opened on a particular day of the week, and went to have a look.
What drew my attention there wasn't all the interesting items for sale,
piled up here and there, but rather how the men in the market looked.
Men who had come out to do food shopping, slowly pulling along
their shopping carts. I felt such a thrill when I noticed men buying this
and that wearing shorts so short they could be swimming trunks.
Wow, would you look at that! Without a care in the world, not thinking
about the gazes of other people, they looked so at ease. I really liked that.

TWO FAMILIAR FIGURES

After coming back to Seoul, I went for a walk around Jongno;
no matter how I searched around and scoured my old memories,
there was nothing familiar. Then finally, from somewhere, I heard a
ringing bell: a sound my ears knew. I could tell what it was right away.
There in the street, with snow swirling all around, stood the
Salvation Army Christmas kettle! Forty years ago, fifty years ago even,
around Christmastime, two people from the Salvation Army would
stand at the junction with Euljiro, ringing a small bell.

It's so wonderful to see them again. Only the color of their clothes
has changed; the sound of the bell is just the same.

Now and then I think that slower is better.

Autumn

WHAT'S HE SO CURIOUS ABOUT?

What's this child so curious about?
It makes me curious, too.
What could he be looking at?
I want to look at it with him.

EACH THEIR OWN

The wind is getting chilly and the clouds are thinning.
It's autumn in São Paulo,
but there are flowers blooming beautifully
in the garden,
even while some trees are dropping their leaves.
I guess the flowers and trees all keep
their own time.

BEFORE TOO LONG

When we were driving along one morning,
I saw a man with bags strapped to his back and hanging from his belt . . .
What could he be thinking about, walking with his head down like that?
Will he be able to put down all those bags and rest before too long?

MY LOVELY ASTRO!

I guess autumn must be in full swing in New York now, too.
This time last year, on our way back to Korea, we spent two weeks with
Astro. Every day we went for walks together to different parks here and
there in the neighborhood. Ripe acorns fell from the oak trees and there
were so many fallen leaves covering the ground that it was all bouncy.
We threw dried leaves up in the air and lay down on them too.
Astro waited, perfectly still, for a squirrel that had gone up a tree,
and when he saw me gathering fallen leaves and putting them in my hat,
he took off his hat and did it, too. My lovely Astro!

In the photograph your mom sent me yesterday,
you were looking at a wild chrysanthemum. Come to think of it,
I visited my old school yesterday and spent a long time looking at the
pale purple asters that had bloomed between rocks . . . Isn't it amazing?
Even though we're far apart, Astro and I were out appreciating nature,
out among the wildflowers of autumn.

We were both looking at wildflowers!

HERE THERE AND EVERYWHERE

Hey, kids,

Do you remember how every Thursday we would all go together to the market near home?

You may have left, but there are things that remind us of you here, there, and everywhere.

SELFIE

Grandpa heard me mumbling, "Taking a selfie isn't as easy as it looks!"
and asked, "Selfie? What's a selfie?" I guess your grandpa didn't
even know the word. I taught him what the word meant, of course,
and also how to take one. He was amazed, saying, "My goodness!
I didn't even know the camera on my phone had a function to make it
so simple." And then right away he exclaimed, "What's so hard about
this?" as he took picture after picture.

What do you kids think? Is Grandpa any good at taking selfies?

After a while, as though he'd made some great discovery,
he looked at me and said, "Ah, now I get it. About selfies . . .
I shouldn't learn from someone who thinks they're difficult."

You kids are going to have to teach us.
On the first day of the New Year, me and Grandpa set a goal:
We want to learn how to take selfies with one hand.
And when we've got that down there will be no stopping us!
We'll take some that look nice and natural and then we can show them off.

BUBBLE WRAP

When we lived in Brazil, there wasn't a nationwide courier system like there is here in Korea. It's amazing! Anything we can think of can be delivered to our door, from art supplies to kimchi, rice, electronics, and even furniture. But it means that we always have loads of Bubble Wrap lying around from the packaging of all the items we order.
I think the Korean word for Bubble Wrap is so fun, *bbok-bbok-i*.
Since it's bad for the environment, we should only order from the courier services when absolutely necessary, but I really love to pop Bubble Wrap. Grandpa always tells me just to throw it away, but I don't care.

Bbok! Bbok! Bbok! Puu-uk!!! Once I get started it's so much fun that I can't pay attention to anything else. But then one day I noticed that Grandpa was drawing me popping Bubble Wrap. He was grumbling about how the transparent surface is hard to draw, and was about to give up and start over when I had a great idea! How about we put a sheet of Bubble Wrap on top of the drawing and then take a picture? And let's upload it with the *bbok bbok bbok* sound, too!

What do you think? Wasn't my idea creative?

DINOSAUR SLIDE

Astro has long loved dinosaurs, and now he finally has a real dinosaur
friend! It looks like he's called over his two cousins to play with him.
He wants to slide down its back, but since he's fond of being silly,
it looks like Astro is trying to slide down at the steepest place.
"Not there! Over this side!" his cousins caution him.

The blue dinosaur, a kind and gentle Brachiosaurus,
that clearly wants to play with these human children,
is standing completely still so that they can play safely.
Wow, it must be so much fun!

FROG FAMILY RIDING A CROCODILE

How nice it was to see our three grandsons on the back of a blue
dinosaur. But what if frogs rode on the back of a crocodile?
In a photograph taken by Tanto Jensen from Jakarta in Indonesia,
a crocodile is giving a ride to a family of frogs! The crocodile waits
until one, two . . . all five frogs have jumped onto its back. The crocodile
waits so patiently, until the entire frog family including a baby frog,
are settled on its back. It should win an award for the best chauffer.

TWO BROTHERS

This is how the boys often appeared to Grandpa walking ahead of him as he accompanied them to and from school when they were in fourth and fifth grade. Walking and talking so close—two boys, one body.

In the way they walk together you can see so clearly exactly what it means to be brothers. Just seeing them like that made us feel content.

Although Arthur was only a year and a half older, he helped Allan with everything. Having his older brother around must have made Allan feel so taken care of!

Arthur would carry his bag for him, and sometimes even play the role of interpreter between Allan and Grandpa. "Allan says he needs to go to the toilet . . . Allan says he's thirsty."

And now you're both adjusting well to Korean society, to an unfamiliar environment. Two like one, you always have each other. Bravo, bravo!

HOMELESS DOGS

Today I went to buy a sweater in a department store and as soon as
I saw the place bustling with people I remembered the end-of-year
holidays in Brazil.

It must have been 1981. During our first December in São Paulo
it felt strange to hear Christmas carols filling the streets in the middle
of summer. It was so different to the kind of Christmas I knew.
But when I saw lots of homeless people lying in the park or on the
street, I was glad that it wasn't cold. When I looked closer, I saw that
most of the homeless had dogs. There were even quite a few who
took care of several.

At around 6:00 pm, they stood in line for dinner that a couple had
prepared for them, and they took their food over to benches where they
sat and shared it with their dogs. Seeing that, I thought, *Oh, of course.
They're like family.*

Why do you think homeless people take care of dogs? To keep them
warm on cold nights? As companions to keep them from feeling lonely?
Or is it because they feel sorry for the dogs who also don't have a home?

SEPARATED FAMILIES

Yesterday a special reunion was held for families who must live apart
in North and South Korea. They were able to meet for a short time at
Mount Kumgang. Among thousands of applicants, less than three
hundred people were selected and allowed to see their family members.
This grandma with a pretty hat is called Lee Geum-seom, and
apparently, she's ninety-two years old. She was separated from her
husband and her four-year-old son more than sixty-five years ago,
while fleeing south during the war. When she saw that son who she lost
so long ago, who she dreamed of all the time, who is now an old man in
his seventies, can you imagine how she felt? How must that mother have
felt when she finally held in her arms the son she could never forget,
who she longed for every day of her life?

Separated by war, they lived their entire lives not even knowing if their
closest family were alive or dead. I can hardly bear to think about all the
wives, husbands, children, and siblings, who remember the last time they
ever set their eyes on their long-lost family, even though they were never
far away. Do you kids know that your grandma's family was also one of
the "separated families," torn apart by war? In Korean the term is *isan
gajok*. It means families who were separated during the Korean War in
the 1950s and ended up on different sides of the armed border that stands
between North and South Korea. To this day, it's almost impossible for
separated families to meet; and even for the lucky ones, it's a bittersweet
one-off chance. I watched the news with tears streaming down my face.

LET'S PLANT APPLE SEEDS

Last week Astro went apple picking with his friend Harin at an
orchard in New Jersey, where autumn is ripening along with the apples.
His parents sent us a photo of Astro picking apples. I'm jealous, Astro.
I was born and grew up in Seoul, so I've never seen an apple orchard
like that. Apparently, Astro also said hello to chickens, llamas, pigs,
and goats on the farm.

Look at all those apples, packed so tightly on the branches.
Were they waiting for you? They're hanging just at your height, Astro,
and it looks as if you are doing a great job picking and filling the basket
with lots of pretty apples. Since you had to stand on tiptoes and reach up
with all your might, the apple you're picking in the picture must have
been one of the more delicious. Aha, now I'm sure you're going to
suggest we plant apple seeds. Let's plant them together, Astro.

MAGPIES

It's been exactly a year since we returned to Korea, although it seems like it's only been a few days since we said our goodbyes at Guarulhos Airport in Brazil. It also seems like it was just a few days ago that we spent a week in New York and played with Astro. And the same goes for the thrill of seeing Arthur and Allan greeting us at Incheon Airport. It's been so good to be able to walk through the autumn streets filled with colorful leaves. And every single day since we got back to Korea, the magpies and their sounds have been bringing us joy.

This morning I opened the apartment window to a bird chirping brightly, and saw a magpie perched on a tree that was changing color. Right in front of my eyes, at the very top of the tallest tree. I don't know whether it was looking for its family or waiting for its friends, but since it perched there perfectly still for a long time, I stayed there observing it. I followed the magpie's gaze and looked out in the same direction. There I saw the beauty of tree leaves changing color moment to moment. And for the first time in ages, I saw a blue sky without a single cloud.

After standing there watching it for a long time, the thought occurred to me, maybe the magpie is worrying about the cold winter that is drawing near.

BTS

BTS, the Bangtan Boys, even their name is ingenious. This group of seven Korean young men are receiving an explosion of love from the whole world for their songs and dancing. Seeing the images of young Americans staying up all night in the street for days on end to buy concert tickets, and their cheers, and the way they sing along, it reminds me of the Beatles in the 1960s. But what makes BTS different is that their fan club, called the ARMY, protect them devotedly with their love. Grandpa is trying to learn the Bangtan Boys' "DNA" dance from his grandsons. There's no way it can go well. But still, Arthur, you said to him, "There's no rush, just do what I do."

SUNFLOWER

Sunflowers always make me think of our early days here in Brazil.
One night, when I couldn't get to sleep, with the television glowing
brightly, I flicked through the channels endlessly, even though I didn't
know any Portuguese. After a while, I came across two faces I knew,
two Italian actors: Sophia Loren and Marcello Mastroianni.

I started watching the film feeling as though I was watching old friends.
It was so beautiful and so sad. The film hadn't been screened in Korea,
so I didn't know anything about this classic by the famous director
Vittorio De Sica. Without being able to understand a single line of the
dialogue, or read even a word of the subtitles, I cried my eyes out till
the very end. The film was *Sunflower* and I only found out later that the
reason it didn't make it onto Korean movie screens was because the
sunflower was the national flower of Russia, and the film included
many scenes shot there. Now it's become a film I will never forget.
Perhaps I cried so much that night because the stifled wail of the woman
in the film who lost her love opened the floodgates of my loneliness,
a loneliness every immigrant feels.

I MISS YOU SO MUCH

Arthur, weren't you born in the year of the monkey? My goodness
you are twelve years old now. It's already a year since you left Brazil.
It's incredible to me that we can talk most days via video call.
What an amazing world we live in. Well, for you video calling might
feel pretty normal, but for your grandpa, the more I think about it
the more grateful and amazed I am.

It must have been a shock to arrive in such an unfamiliar place.
I bet Korea's really different than Brazil. Everyone is always in such a
hurry in Korea; it won't be as simple for you to go at your nice and
relaxed pace there. But try not to rush everything; take time to look
around instead of always looking out ahead.

I'm glad to hear that you've started playing baseball; you never got to
try it in Brazil. And it's great that you have lunch at the school canteen
with your friends and go on field trips to the museum and observatory.
More than anything, I'm glad your school is just across the road from
your home, so you can walk to school with your younger brother,
just the two of you. These days, your grandpa keeps thinking back
over the five years when I took you to and from school. Did you know
that every time you'd giggle away in the backseat, I was laughing along
with you at the steering wheel? I miss those times so much.

It's morning here, and I'm about to go to the park to get some exercise. You're probably in bed asleep. Maybe we'll be able to meet in dreamland. Sleep well, sweet dreams . . .

STEAMING HOT CORN

Is there anyone who doesn't like boiled corn?
In Brazil, people enjoy the corn sold at roadside stalls no matter what
the season. Today, on my way to visit a friend, I was hurrying along the
street when I noticed that tasty smell of boiled corn. With the weather
turning colder, "Ah!" I thought, "What a great idea!" and I looked
around to see a whole row of corn sellers. I picked a handcart run by
an old man, and as soon as I approached, his face lit up.

"I'll take three please. Nice soft ones, with just a little bit of salt,
and a touch of margarine."

The old man looked for a good one and then he placed it on a long leaf
and seasoned it carefully with salt and margarine. Seeing how earnestly
he worked and what a good job he was doing, I ordered one extra
even though I only needed two. Just when I said it, what's this?
He went and picked out a fourth one!

When I said, "Oh no, that's OK. Three is plenty," the man gave me a big
smile and said, "The last one's a gift."

Enjoying the still-warm corn with my friend, I realized that sharing
steaming hot corn makes it even more delicious.

CHEETAH

All children like animals, don't they?
To tell the truth, I'm no animal expert.
I looked up in a book what animals we have in Brazil
that can't be found in Korea.
There are leopards and cheetahs in Brazil but none in Korea.
Ah, how are those two different again?

Grandpa starts drawing a cheetah for me.
I watch closely from the sidelines as he paints it with a vibrant pattern.
The slim cheetah runs with all its strength.
I can hear its labored breath from here.

THREE BABIES

Three babies, lying side by side, communicating with their hands
and feet: Bernardo, Olivia, and Christian.

The babies' grandparents all immigrated to Brazil in the 1970s and had
sons around the same time. Their children all got married around the
same time and had babies of their own a month apart. Third-generation
Korean Brazilians. Seeing their cute round faces, you can clearly tell
that they're Korean, can't you? Look at their arms and legs squirming,
never still for a moment. I can feel their drive to explore those two
countries. No, to explore the whole world.

THOMAS AND FRIENDS

The moment I saw the pretty tourist train in Paranapiacaba,
I thought of Allan. Allan, you loved everything with wheels.
You'd lie down flat on your stomach to get a better look at the wheels
of any toy that had them. And you'd push little cars along so slowly,
paying close attention to how the wheels spun. Your grandma knows
just how thoroughly you researched wheels. Your number one treasure
was the Thomas and Friends toy set that your uncle sent you.
Every time you recited for me the names of each and every one of
Thomas's friends, I really tried to memorize them, but I never managed it.

OLD MAN PLAYING THE ACCORDION

I heard a faint melody as I passed by Tiradentes Station. It was a really foreign sound. An old man was playing an accordion, but it was very, very quiet. So much so that, if he hadn't been moving his hands and fingers, I would not have been sure the music was coming from his instrument. Maybe he was just a statue that had been there for years. The accordion was very small and looked lightweight. The color of it was interesting, too. But it wasn't just the instrument that was unique.

The bandana the old man was wearing, his long white beard, and the color of his clothes were all peculiar, too, as though he had just arrived from some distant land. The bundles piled high beside him were unusual, too. Most people just walked past him indifferently, but I sat down on a bench nearby to study him slowly.

The first thing I noticed was that all of his things were made of paper! The accordion, his bandana, and his scarf, too, it was all made of paper. His small paper instrument was made to create melodies, making sounds when a certain place was pressed. Looking at thev bundles beside him, I could picture how the old man spent his days. If Brazilian writer José Mauro de Vasconcelos had seen him, I'm sure he would have written the old man's story as a sequel to *My Sweet Orange Tree*.

200

HE MUST HAVE SLIPPED SOFTLY
OFF TO SLEEP

How exhausted this man must have been, he was totally unaware of me
approaching and just continued sleeping. It looks as though he collects
wastepaper, doesn't it? He's not someone I know but someone I saw as
I was out walking. The sight of him having fallen asleep in his own
place looked so peaceful somehow . . .

Listening to music, he must have slipped softly off to sleep.
I slowed my steps as I passed by him, trying hard not to make a sound.

TCHAU, BRAZIL!

We passed by this place almost every morning for thirty-six years,
driving along the main road. Going through the Anhangabaú tunnel
was the only way to get to the Bom Retiro district, where we worked.
The Brazilian flag that fluttered high up there was what first greeted us
from far away. How can we ever forget that sight? It felt like it was
cheering us on, always there in the same spot, no matter what
the weather. And now I'm sure it will bless our future days
as we leave this land.

Oh, Brazil, we are so grateful you took us in, weak as we were,
in your kind embrace, and now it's time to say goodbye.

Goodbye!
Oh, Brazil of shining azure, goodbye!
And, just one more thing before we go,
Long Live Brazil!

Grandpa Thinking of his Parents

A MEMORY OF MY FATHER

In January 1951, during the Korean War, my family had to
leave Seoul in the dead of winter to escape the fighting.
Having walked all day long without saying a word, at night we
refugees had to sleep, but there was no shelter for us anywhere.
We stopped for the night in a snow-covered field. My father laid
me on top of him so I wouldn't have to sleep on the cold ground.
When that night comes back to me from time to time, I mumble
to myself: "Why didn't I realize then, Father, how cold and tired
you must have been? I was eight years old. I should have known!
Why is that night so deeply embedded in my memory?"

WHAT DYING MEANS

Do you kids know what death is? I think I was about four or five
when I first heard about dying. One day, my parents told me, simply,
"People die."

"Will you die, too?" As soon as I heard them say that they would,
I got so worked up I burst into tears. I can still remember vividly
how I cried that day, even now that I'm over seventy.
Did I cry like that because I understood what dying means?
I was so young then, why did it make me so sad?

FATHER MAKING SOCCER BOOTS

I've tried to draw my father. Your great-grandfather was a soccer player
since before your grandpa was born. Even when he stopped playing,
he kept working as a coach and as a manager, so you could say that he
was a historic figure in Korean soccer. He was renowned for his skill at
making soccer boots, too, so he got lots of group orders. People called
him "old tobacco pipe man" because he had his pipe in his mouth even
when he was hammering away at the boots he made that fit the players'
feet perfectly. When I was in middle school, father was constantly
working at making soccer boots, but our family was very poor.
In the old days soccer players were poor, so they had shoes made,
but then they couldn't pay. If father happened to spot one of those
soccer players approaching as he walked down the street, he would
change course to avoid them. He knew how sorry they must feel.
We were all so poor in the 1950s!

MOTHER

Back when I was in high school, more than fifty years ago now,
I came home one day and, just like I did every day, I opened the door
to the main room to greet my mother. But Mother was lying in bed,
with the aunties from the neighborhood sitting all around her.
I was really worried, because Mother never laid down in the daytime,
but I just thought to myself, *Oh, Mom's sick! She must be really sick,*
and closed the door again without saying a word.

Years later, Mother told her daughter-in-law about that day.
She said that she knew her son wasn't a big talker, but she was really
disappointed, and it made her very sad. "Well, Chan Jae just took
one look at me and shut the door." I'm still not great at expressing my
emotions, but I'm getting better at it now that I have you grandchildren.

"Are you hurt? Do you need medicine? It's okay, you'll feel better after
a hug from Grandpa."

Remembering that day when I was a boy, I feel like my heart might
burst. If only I could still beg for her forgiveness now, though even
that would be too late.

NEW YEAR MONEY POUCH

I can still remember one particular Lunar New Year when I received New Year's pocket money. Every time I gave a big bow and received money, I placed it neatly in a pretty pouch, and it made me so inexpressibly happy. The next morning, as soon as I opened my eyes, I searched for the pouch that was under my pillow. It was there, but it felt flat. I hurriedly opened the pouch and found that it was completely empty. I think the shock I felt in that moment was similar to fear. I went and told my mom, but she wasn't shocked at all, she simply said calmly: "I'm looking after your New Year's money for you. I'll take good care of it and give it back when you're older."

I couldn't bring myself to argue with what she said, and for some reason I couldn't cry, either. Why was that? I probably knew somehow that I wasn't ever going to get that money back. I may have been young, but I knew why Mom had to take it. All the same, I could have cried. I could at least have cried.

Our family was poor. So poor that I knew it even though I was young. I knew that crying would be no use, that I mustn't cry. Do you know what it means to be poor, kids? I still can't forget how that pouch felt that morning. A flat pouch, an empty pouch. My pretty pouch, totally empty.

Just like that, we find ourselves missing you.

Winter

TAKE A LOOK AT THIS CHILD

Look at this child's pose.
Is he sleeping, you ask?
Yes. He's sleeping.
Can you feel that he suddenly became so tired from running around
that he just stopped in his tracks?
Take a look at his butt sticking out.
Can you see that he's completely exhausted himself having fun?
Look at his arms tucked under his chest.

An exhausted child napping sweetly on the ground,
once he's had a quick sleep, he'll wake up and cry out, "Mo-om!"

A MOTHER'S HEART

In the waiting room at the doctors, I saw a young mother with her baby
beside her in a stroller. She was peering in and speaking softly to her
child. Inside a stroller with a clear window in the cover, the baby sat
still, staring back at their mom. They both looked ill and it was
heartrending to see the mom as she looked at her suffering baby.

Then I remembered the time I hugged my own baby to my chest
and he was boiling with a fever. I rushed to the local doctor. There was
a strong wind and snow was falling in thick sheets to the ground.
I can still recall the terror I felt when the doctor said I had to take him
to a bigger clinic. It must have been 1973. He's a father himself now,
but I never told my son this story. That's right, son, your mother's heart
nearly fell out of her chest worrying about you.

My turn was called and I got my prescription for blood-pressure
medication. As I was coming out of the doctor's office, I looked again
at the mother and baby. The baby was smiling. And the mom was
smiling, too. They were smiling at each other. So I was able to leave
the doctors smiling, too.

It was the middle of winter, on a really cold morning.

SANTA CLAUS

Hey, Astro, did you have a fun Christmas?

Would you look at this young Santa Claus speeding along on skis.

I thought that Santa Claus came riding on a sleigh, but I guess things are different these days. There must be more well-behaved children than there used to be. So Santa has to prepare more gifts, and to reach all the children waiting for him before Christmas morning, he must have entrusted his happy work to young people who are good skiers.

Hey, Astro, you didn't pout or cry, so you must have gotten loads of gifts. I'll have to ask Arthur and Allan, too.

THE CRY OF A MAGPIE

There's something that really made me feel like I was back home when we returned to Korea. You see, the very first day we moved in, I heard a familiar sound coming from the forest that surrounds our apartment complex. It was the cry of a magpie, the first time I'd heard it in thirty-six years. The sound hadn't changed a bit.

In this picture magpies are sitting on a persimmon tree, calling to their friends as they busily peck at the fruits. In the olden days, people in rural villages didn't pick all of the persimmons. They left some as food for the magpies who wouldn't have had enough to eat during the harsh cold winter if they hadn't. Apparently, magpies, who once felt like friends, are now a real nuisance for fruit growers. Why did the magpies end up pecking at the fruit in orchards? They never did that in the olden days. I guess there are fewer wild trees now.

NEW YEAR'S BOW

Astro, not yet two years old, bowed to Grandma and Grandpa on New Year's morning. He even wore a proper *hanbok*. He must have learned how to do a New Year's bow from his mom. "Bow to your grandparents, Astro! You can do it." His mom and dad encourage him, and Astro bows right down onto his hands and knees. As he does it, as though not sure he's getting it right, he turns his head a little and looks at his mom. As though asking, *This is how I'm supposed to do it, right?*

Watching him, I feel so proud I don't know what to do. Next year he'll be able to bow confidently all on his own, and by then I guess he'll be able to say, *Saehae bok mani badeuseyo*, to wish us good luck in the year ahead. Then we'll tell him this: "Our lovely Astro, we wish you good luck, too! Oh, let's not forget, we have to give you some pocket money!"

GRANDPA SLEEPING

Hey, kids, the more I think about it, the more strange things there are in this life. You must be wondering what I mean. Well, you know your grandpa and I are very different, so it's amazing to me how well we've lived together for more than fifty years. Your grandpa loves spending time with friends, but he's never the one to pick up the phone to say let's go somewhere or do something. But compared to your grandpa, I'm pretty good at that. It's always me who organizes trips to the seaside in summer, trips to the countryside in autumn, and spending time with friends and their families. Unlike me, your grandpa has no interest in plants, and he's an early riser, whereas I always like to sleep late. Well, I don't know if it's because it's winter now, or if my sleeping late is contagious, but every so often these days your grandpa sleeps in past 8:00 am, too. One morning after waking up late, he said with wonder in his voice, "So this is what all the fuss was about!"

AGING FRIENDS

For both me and your grandpa, it's a real joy to meet up with friends
and chat about this and that. Yesterday Grandpa went out to meet his
university friends. They're all old men approaching eighty now.
Apparently one of them is starting to have issues. Even though they
always meet at the same place, and despite the fact that the organizer
of the group always calls him the day before to remind him to meet at
Yeongdeungpo District Office Station, nine times out of ten he goes
to Yeongdeungpo Station instead.

Apparently, after the meeting yesterday, this friend and one other
followed Grandpa, saying "Oi, Chan Jae! Let's go to Incheon for
another round of drinks!" If it was back in the old days he would have
agreed in an instant, but now he should only drink in moderation.
But according to Grandpa, there was no way to refuse their invitation.
So, at the subway station, he hid from them behind a pillar!
Spying from a distance as his friends looked all around searching
for him, he became really sad.

"The passionate young physics teacher who used to go on and on
about Einstein had disappeared . . . Now my friends have become
hunched-over old men. Looking at them, it occurred to me that
I must look like that, too."

Hearing your grandpa lamenting like that made me feel sad as well.

EYEBROWS

This morning your grandpa was mumbling away to himself, "I didn't really know what aging was. I just lived day after day without giving it a thought. But these days I've been noticing some changes in my body."

His first discovery was his eyebrows! Now that the hair on his head is white, it's much softer. But his eyebrows are really thick and long and stick straight out as stiff as wires. "It seems as if everything I eat goes into growing my eyebrows," Grandpa mumbles as he tries to trim them himself, looking in the mirror, but then he gives up and asks me to take over.

In the end I did trim them for him, but even though I was wearing my glasses, I couldn't see that well, so I got told off for not being neat enough.

This old couple's morning routine is just plain funny these days.

234

LOOK OVER THERE!

I told you, didn't I, that there's a really good place to go climbing
on the outskirts of São Paulo? It's called Atibaia, and I discovered
something fun in the photograph a friend sent me from there today.
Everyone in the photograph is raising their hand to point at something,
and they are all pointing in the same direction. What did they see?
What was it that caught their attention?

KO, KO, KO

Astro is learning Korean from Grandpa.

"What's nose, Astro?"

"*Ko!*"

"What about mouth?"

"*Ip!*"

"And ears?"

"*Gwi!*"

"And forehead?"

"*Ima!*"

Now they play a game and Astro is in charge.

"*Ko, ko, ko . . . ip!*"

"*Ko, ko, ko . . . gwi!*"

"*Ko, ko, ko . . . ima!*"

He keeps poking Grandpa's nose with his forefinger and then suddenly touches his ear and shouts, "Mouth!"

If Grandpa follows suit and touches his ear, he's out.

He has to point to his mouth. This game for learning words has come down through generations!

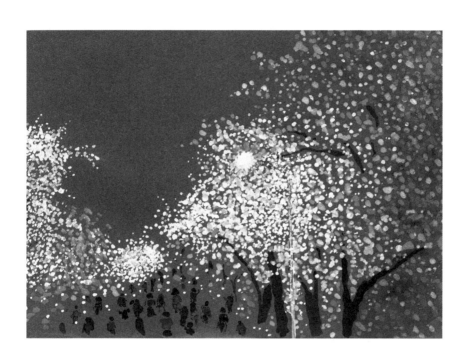

CHERRY BLOSSOMS BY NIGHT

Winter was long and cold. At the first hint that winter might be retreating, the cherry blossoms appear without a sound. They bloom all together in an instant as if to make up for the fact that they will disappear so soon. Because we know we'll soon have to say goodbye to them, we light up the trees and skip sleep to walk beneath them all night long.

GRANDMA'S GRADUATION PHOTO

Do you want to hear a story of when your grandpa was doing his military service in a missile unit in Busan? I sent him my university graduation photo, with me wearing a mortarboard. Grandpa kept the photo inside his uniform cap and kept looking at it in secret whenever he had the chance. I remember he wrote to me in a letter that no matter how hard the training was, what unfair punishment he received, that photo always comforted him and gave him courage. But then! One day the photo that was in his cap disappeared! He said he thought he would go crazy. Can you imagine how desperate he must have felt? What made him most anxious was the thought that some other soldier was enjoying looking at my pretty face and not him. Well, here it is! Your grandma, freshly graduated in February 1965! Don't I look all bright and innocent?

THE CUTEST ROYAL GUARD

A tiny royal guard stands next to the official guard on duty
for the royal family. Isn't the sight of them standing together so cute?

The little boy wanted to go to Windsor Castle for his fourth birthday
to say hello to the queen, so his mother dressed him up in a red royal
guard costume. That day, the young son and his mother were perfectly
in tune. The grandmother queen who receives so much love from her
people must have given special notice to the little boy as he saluted her
with all his might. It's all just so beautiful!

A CHALLENGE IS NEVER EASY

One day, Allan asked Grandpa to teach him how to draw pictures on the iPad. I listened carefully from the sidelines, waiting to see what would happen. "Ah, really? You want to learn?"

I was nervous. You see, I knew that Grandpa hadn't even turned on the iPad for ages. What if he couldn't remember how to use it and got all flustered?

Fortunately, Grandpa was able to teach you without a single hesitation. In fact, it was you, Allan, who had to rush to keep up. To tell you the truth, new challenges are hard for older people. We keep forgetting. Someday, when Grandpa can't remember and starts struggling, that's when you can come in to save the day and teach *him* instead!

THE LIFE OF A STRAY CAT

In a deserted old neighborhood that is crumbling away, there sits a cat.
The neighborhood is about to be redeveloped. The old buildings are
dangerous now, so they have to be knocked down and the people who
used to live there have had to leave. There's no one feeding the cat now.
There isn't even any trash, and no trash means no mice . . . All that's left
are lonely, hungry cats. It makes me feel so grateful to see that there are
people who come to feed the stray cats that cry with hunger on a cold day.

I remember the old saying "Cats don't follow people like dogs do,
they stay where they have always lived." Was it my now-deceased
mother who taught me that? I think so.

WAYS OF LOOKING AT PICTURES

"Look at this! They're all the same."

Two-year-old Astro points at a series of paintings on the wall.
What you must have wanted to say was
"Why are there so many identical things like this?"
You were wondering, *Why did someone paint the same thing over and over?*
How strange. Although plenty of adults might find it strange, too, they
don't question it. Astro doesn't hold back from saying what he thinks.

We can't wait to hear what you'll say when you're five.
And what about when you're fifteen?

CHUGGA-CHUGGA, CHUGGA-CHUGGA

Astro is playing trains today. "Chugga-chugga, chugga-chugga,
toot toot!" And it looks like he's just come up with a great idea.
He starts making a train out of dinosaur figures.
Do you think he thought of it because he has so many?

"That looks like fun!" says Grandpa. "I want to play at making trains
too! I'll make a train of my own and show it to Astro." Grandpa makes
a train out of Astro's shoes. The train of shoes keeps getting longer.
A red shoe, a green shoe, a yellow shoe . . . Now the pretty shoe train
is ready for departure. Where will it go?

Astro is still making his train. It's getting longer and longer.
And he still has a few more T. rexes.

251

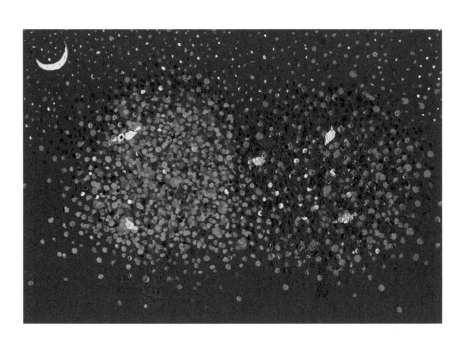

WHERE DO BIRDS SLEEP?

Where do all the birds in our neighborhood sleep at night?
Why don't children ask this?
Do they know already?
In the apartment complex where we live there are as many trees
as there are units.
If you look down from our apartment at night all you can see
is dark forest.
I'm reminded of a line from an old poem: When morning comes
birds leave the tree, and at nightfall they gather again.
I've never actually seen it so I don't know for sure, but I believe
that birds sleep in the trees.
In their little forest with stars shining brightly in the sky overhead,
I imagine they fall asleep after telling each other about their day.
I hope they sleep carefree in the quiet darkness . . .

A SEA OF QUARESMEIRA

Grandpa has drawn the flowering trees that greet you everywhere
you go in February in São Paulo. Light pink, magenta, purple . . .
different-colored flowers bloom together on one tree. But the flowers are
all the same shape, only the color is different. It amazes me every time I
see them. They are called quaresmeira. The name comes from *quaresma*,
which means "lent" in Portuguese, because that's when they bloom, at
the time when people think about the death and resurrection of Jesus.

Once, we went up to Paranapiacaba near São Paulo, and from the top
of the mountain we looked out and over to the other side and there was
a whole mountain covered with quaresmeira. A sea of beautiful flowers,
laid out beneath the sky. It was such a majestic and breathtaking view.
I'd never seen anything like it. It's vivid in my mind's eye even now,
as if it were right in front of me.

DEAR LUA

A Letter from Your Grandpa

When I held out my hand to you, you grabbed one of my fingers.
You grabbed it with all five of your fingers and held it
with all your strength. It seemed like you'd never let me go.

When I first felt your strength in my finger I couldn't stop myself from
tearing up. Your hand was tiny, but the strength of it was immense.
You grabbed my whole body, my whole heart, with the strength
in your tiny plump hand!

When you held on to me, at that very moment, my heart cried out,
Yes, little baby. Don't you worry. Your grandpa is here.

STRING OF HEARTS

This is the String of Hearts I planted in our apartment veranda.
Even the name is lovely, don't you think? I think it was in 1979.
A friend of mine lived in Tokyo for a few years and learned flower
arranging there; she even got a qualification in it. When she returned to
Seoul, I went to visit her home, and she gave me a cutting from this cute
vine called String of Hearts. I planted it as soon as I got home and
looked after it, and little by little it started to put down roots. Just like
the name, the leaves were heart shaped. We ended up leaving for Brazil
not long after that, and I gave the String of Hearts away to a neighbor.

Once we'd arrived and settled down in São Paulo and I had a bit more
time on my hands, I spotted a String of Hearts in a hanging basket at a
flower shop. Coming across this familiar plant made me incredibly happy.
Who knew they had String of Hearts so very far away! I bought the plant
right away, and on my way back home I thought of the word *fate*.

The String of Hearts was growing well in no time, and then it started
flowering. On every string, where the flowers had been, there appeared
little berry-type things the size of beans, that Brazilians call "potatoes."
When I picked them and planted them in a new pot another vine would
grow. I did this over and over, until I had loads of them. I shared them
with all of our neighbors when we were returning to Korea, and a couple
of months ago I got a message from one of them saying that the String of
Hearts I gave them is growing well. It gave me such a feeling of delight.

259

ON ALL SOULS' DAY

I'm pretty sure Arthur was in fourth grade when we took the two of you to Cemitério Gethsêmani in São Paulo. There were lots of Brazilian people there because it was All Souls' Day. It was hot, but the breeze was nice and cool. With brightly colored flowers arranged by every grave, the shadow of death was nowhere to be found. We laughed together as we picked the weeds around the grave for my family, and polished the nameplate with my parents' names engraved into it.
We polished it until it glistened. And then we lit incense and poured a cup of wine as an offering to them. We put our hands together and lowered our heads to bow and pay our respects. Even you boys poured a cup and placed it by the grave for your great-grandparents.
I explained to you that when my parents died they were buried here, and that they were laying beneath the ground. I carried on and said, "When we die, your grandma and grandpa will be buried here, too."

I just came out with it. Well, actually, I really wanted you to know. You were still young, but I wanted to tell you then because the sky was clear that day and everyone around us was moving with care, and the flowers at all the graves were so beautiful.

But it seems you were shocked by what you heard, that your grandpa and grandma would die one day and be buried.

"Grandpa and Grandma will die, too?"

"Of course. Everyone dies eventually."

Later I heard that when Arthur got home and told his mom about our trip to the graveyard he asked if it was really true, that Grandma and Grandpa would die and be buried in the ground.

IT WAS IN MY HEART ALL ALONG

When we first arrived in Brazil and were looking around for a home,
I discovered something amazing. I really want to tell you about it.
Would you believe that there could be a graveyard right in the middle of
a residential neighborhood? We were being shown around an apartment
on a high floor of a tall building by a real estate agent, and I got a real
fright when I looked out of the window. Right below the apartment
there was an area of green with lots of trees. I thought it must be a park,
but it wasn't. It was a graveyard, right in the heart of São Paulo,
something that would never happen in Seoul.

The first time I went to pay my respects at a wake in Brazil, I saw people
kissing the face and touching the hands of the deceased in the coffin.
Perhaps for the mourners there was nothing separating the living
and the dead, or perhaps it was just that their understanding of death
was different to mine, but I was in shock for quite a while.

Now, having lived in Brazil for decades, when I go to pay my respects,
I always make sure to go up to the coffin and look at the deceased's face.
Somehow it doesn't feel strange anymore. I know now that it was all
in my heart already. My heart is what guides me to draw closer.
Feeling afraid of death was just something that I learned;
it didn't come from inside me. Well, now I've learned a new way of
understanding death from my friends in Brazil.

As soon as we see flowers burst into bloom . . .

As soon as we see a dandelion growing by the path on our way home . . .

Just like that, we find ourselves missing you.
Your grandpa and grandma, we are always thinking of you.
Every moment.

AFTERWORD

Come What May, Life Is Still Beautiful

I'm sure that, years from now, our grandchildren will find themselves thinking of their grandma and grandpa every so often. I imagine those times, now and then, when they will look at their grandpa's drawings with their grandma's words written beside them and feel peaceful and loved.

Perhaps they will think to themselves such things as: *Grandpa and Grandma were children once, too. They lived through a war. They even had to seek refuge! They say that Grandpa always liked to sing, so I still don't understand why he wouldn't learn the songs of the girl bands and boy bands we liked. So that's what I was like when I was little. I didn't know I played with Grandma and Grandpa so much . . .*

Pretending as though I'm not looking, I study my husband's face as he draws. My husband, whose laughter lines are growing deeper, and whose hair is now completely white. My husband, who can't hear well even with his hearing aid, so his favorite things to watch on television are billiards games and *baduk* matches. But he's a mysterious husband, who, despite being hard of hearing, knows all about what's going on in South Korea, North Korea, America, China, Japan, Russia, Brazil, and all over the world. As I watch my husband get older, I've started to believe that saying about how people become holy as they age. You, dear, are the household god that guards our home.

We worked hard in Brazil. We never shirked any duty. All of the people who shopped at our store were Brazilian, and we were so grateful to each and every one of them. Brazil is full of kind, warmhearted people. People who understand you even if you struggle with the language, and who rush to help if someone falls and hold their arms and bring water for them to drink, and who are so good at expressing their gratitude. People in Brazil never give judgmental, sidelong glances. And all that meant we were able to be happy there.

Many people have said to me, "Doesn't it feel wonderful to be back home after thirty-six years?" But my home isn't anywhere now. Well, maybe not exactly. It's more like, now, I have more places that feel like home. Seoul is home to me, and Tongyeong, too, and Busan and São Paulo, and Bucheon, where we live now. They are all my home in a way. And Pakchŏn, my ancestral hometown in Pyongan Province, made so much farther away by the DMZ, is a very old, faint home of mine, too.

There are also people who ask "Why did you come back to Korea?" The truth is, I don't know. Why did we come back to Korea after living in

Brazil for half our lives? There must be a reason, they say. But there isn't. Some things in life don't have a reason.

Sometimes pain and suffering come along, with one thing following another, like terrible waves crashing in succession. There are times when I'm even afraid of going to sleep, of waking up in the morning. There are times when I don't want to see anybody, when the idea of meeting people scares me. When that happens, with the help of my family and friends, and with the help of time, all that fear starts to melt away. So, above all, the place where there are people who will say "What's wrong? Who did this?" and stand up for me, the place I can call my own, the place where my family is, that's home to me.

I decided to take a break from writing. I put on a pretty colored scarf and my new jeans and left the house. I was planning to go to the doctors to ask, "I'm having trouble getting to sleep, what should I do?" There were lots of children out in the park. The sight of them running here and there and laughing and frolicking around filled me with a sense of peace. Then one child let out a shriek and started to cry.

Where are they? Who is it? What happened? Suddenly I became anxious. Five or six children were huddled together; one wiping the crying child's tears, one rubbing her knee and comforting her with "It's alright. It's not bleeding." Then the group of children all got up and started running around again. There were bursts of laughter and it was hard to tell which one of them had just been crying. I sat for a long time on a bench watching the children, and then, I just came back home. I'd forgotten all about going to the doctors.

The sound of children laughing makes everyone happy. If people hear children's laughter when they're feeling depressed or beyond hope, it can make them forget all their troubles. Do you children know that? Your clear and bright laughter can make those who are alone forget their loneliness and help to heal the most terrible pain. Sadly, there are too many times when we forget what a mysterious power the sound of your laughter has. But I shouldn't be worrying about that. You are always laughing! All the same, let's remind ourselves now and then how important laughter is in life.

Having our story bound into a book feels pretty strange. All of a sudden, I can look back over our life spread out across the pages. At the time, making it through each day we were faced with felt like such an unbearable challenge, and life just seemed exhausting. Each day was another hill to climb. But looking back from where I stand now, each and every one of those moments was beautiful. They were radiant. Despite it all, life was beautiful. I really wanted to tell you that.

1968

2019

ABOUT THE AUTHORS

Grandpa Chan (Chan Jae Lee)—Illustrator
Born in Seoul in 1942, he graduated from the earth science department at Seoul National University's College of Education and worked as an earth science teacher. After moving to Brazil he ran a clothing business. He has held exhibitions of his drawings in San José, Costa Rica; São Paulo, Brazil; and in Seoul, Korea.

Grandma Marina (Kyong Ja An)—Writer
Born in Seoul in 1942, she graduated from the Korean language education department at Seoul National University's College of Education and worked as a Korean teacher. After moving to Brazil, while working in the family clothing business, she served as the principal of the Korean language school in São Paulo and taught Korean literature at an international school.

And together . . .

The two married at the age of twenty-five and had one son and one daughter. In 1981, they immigrated to São Paulo, Brazil. When their two grandsons Arthur and Allan moved to Korea with their daughter and son-in-law in 2015, they began drawing pictures and writing words to post on Instagram as a productive pastime. Then when their third grandson, Astro, was born to their son living in New York, the grandparents started to draw and write for their three grandchildren. Before long, their letters touched the hearts of people all around the world and they received interest and praise from major international media outlets such as the BBC, NBC, and the *Guardian*. They currently have 400,000 Instagram followers from all over the world encouraging their work.

In October 2017 they ended their thirty-six-year sojourn in Brazil and returned to Korea for good, to be reunited with Arthur and Allan, and they travel to New York as often as they can to see Astro and his new sister, Lua. And wherever they go, they still draw and write and share their work with the world.

About the translator

Sophie Bowman was born and grew up in London. After graduating from university, she moved to Seoul, where she lived, worked, married, and studied, for seven years before moving to Toronto in 2018, where she translates and researches Korean literature.

ACKNOWLEDGMENTS

A new book is born.

A child, a piece of art, a book . . . All births come with pain, patience, conflicts, expectations, and joy. And we think about all those who gave their love to make this birth possible.

First, we thank our family. Our son, Ji, and our daughter, Miru, and our four grandchildren, Arthur, Allan, Astro, and Lua, who encourage and inspire us every day.

We thank all the fans who have been cheering for us with their hearts like a family. You give us the strength to keep moving forward.

We thank Suo Books who first published our book in Korea in 2019 and made it so beautiful.

We thank TarcherPerigee who published this book. We thank our editor, Sara Carder, who believed in our work and collaborated closely with us in every step from the beginning to the end. We thank our translator, Sophie Bowman. We know how much time and effort went into translating our Korean text into English. Special thanks to Sara Johnson, Anne Kosmoski, Alex Casement, and the TarcherPerigee publicity and marketing team. We thank the coordinator, Rachel Ayotte, the designers, Linet Huaman Velázquez, Lorie Pagnozzi, and Laura Corless who worked very hard to make our book beautiful.

Thank you.

Grandpa Chan & Grandma Marina

또다른 옷을 입고 또다른 모습으로 이제 한 권의 책이 탄생합니다.

모든 탄생은,

그것이 어린 생명이든 예술작품이든 책이든

고통과 인내와 갈등과 기대와 환희를 함께 합니다.

그래서 이 탄생을 위해 사랑을 주신 이들이 떠오르는 것입니다.

무엇보다 우리 식구들이 고맙습니다.

또 식구처럼 한결같은 마음으로 응원을 보내주고 있는 팬 여러분, 고맙습니다. 당신들이 있기에 이렇게 씩씩하게 걸어오고 있답니다.

아, 아름다운 책을 만들어주신 한국의 <수오서재>에게 인사를 드립니다.

그리고 번역해준 소피, 언어와 언어 사이에서 얼마나 애쓰셨을지 잘 압니다. 너무도 고맙습니다.

이제 이 작은 책이 세계 더 많은 이들을 찾아가도록 고민하고 고민하신 펭귄 여러분, 고맙습니다. 책을 만드는 것은 얼마나 아름다운 일입니까? 수고 많으셨습니다.